OSCARS

2025

HIGHLIGHTS

CW01497434

PAUL ZILLMAN

OSCARS 2025 HIGHLIGHTS

ISBN: 9798312938821

CONTENTS

OSCARS 2025 HIGHLIGHTS

Introduction

The Academy Awards, better known as the Oscars, are more than just a night of glamour and celebration. They represent a tradition deeply woven into the fabric of Hollywood, shaping careers, influencing film trends, and sparking conversations that extend far beyond the industry. Every year, audiences worldwide tune in to watch their favorite actors, directors, and creators take the stage, hoping to see history made. But beneath the dazzling gowns, emotional speeches, and golden statuettes lies a competition that reflects the state of modern cinema, highlighting the evolution of storytelling, technology, and cultural impact.

The 97th Academy Awards were no different. From the moment the nominations were announced, debates ignited over who deserved recognition, who was overlooked, and what the final results would mean for the future of film. As the biggest night in Hollywood approached, anticipation built around major categories, surprise contenders, and the inevitable moments that would dominate social media and headlines. The Oscars have long been a barometer of artistic excellence, but they also serve as a reflection of the changing tides in the entertainment industry. Whether it's a groundbreaking indie film rising above big-budget blockbusters or a long-overdue artist finally receiving their due, every ceremony adds a new chapter to its history.

Beyond the winners and nominees, the Oscars are a spectacle that blends artistry with entertainment. The host's monologue sets the tone for the evening, the performances bring a mix of energy and emotion, and the acceptance speeches range from heartfelt to political. Controversies and surprises are just as much a part of the tradition as the awards themselves. Over the years, the ceremony has evolved to embrace new voices, new formats, and even new challenges, from navigating industry strikes to addressing diversity concerns. With streaming services challenging traditional studios and audiences demanding more representation, the Oscars remain at the center of discussions about where the film industry is headed.

OSCARS 2025 HIGHLIGHTS

As we look at the highlights of this year's ceremony, it's clear that the Oscars are more than just a celebration of the best in film. They are a reflection of the times, a conversation starter, and a stage where art and recognition meet. Whether it's a record-breaking win, a career-defining speech, or an unexpected moment that captures the world's attention, the Academy Awards continue to be a night where Hollywood's brightest stars shine, and where the magic of movies is honored in grand fashion.

OSCARS 2025 HIGHLIGHTS

Overview of the 97th Academy Awards

The 97th Academy Awards took place on March 2, 2025, at the Dolby Theatre in Hollywood, Los Angeles. Conan O'Brien hosted the event, bringing his signature humor to the evening.

This year's ceremony stood out for several reasons, particularly its largely apolitical nature, a shift from recent years when social issues were more prominently discussed in speeches.

The nominations were revealed on January 23, 2025, by actors Bowen Yang and Rachel Sennott. Originally set for January 17, the announcement was delayed due to wildfires in Southern California.

OSCARS 2025 HIGHLIGHTS

Lasting about three hours and 50 minutes, the ceremony was broadcast live on ABC, streamed on Hulu, and aired across more than 200 territories worldwide.

The 97th Oscars were notable for their neutral tone, strides in diversity and representation, and a few surprising results, reflecting the film industry's ongoing evolution.

Host and Ceremony Highlights

The 97th Academy Awards were a night filled with unforgettable moments, laughter, and celebration, largely thanks to the choice of host, Conan O'Brien. Hosting the Oscars for the first time, O'Brien brought his signature wit and comedic timing to Hollywood's most prestigious night, proving that the Academy's decision to have him lead the show was a wise one.

From the moment he stepped onto the stage at the Dolby Theatre in Los Angeles, it was clear that the night would be different. O'Brien, known for his quick humor and improvisational skills, set the tone with an opening monologue that blended sharp satire with playful jabs at the entertainment industry. His opening joke, referencing his hosting duties alongside a lighthearted mention of a fast-food promotion, instantly warmed up the audience. "America demanded it, and now it's happening," he quipped. "Taco Bell's new Cheesy Chalupa Supreme. In other news, I'm hosting the Oscars." The crowd erupted in laughter, signaling a night where entertainment would take center stage.

Unlike previous years, where political commentary often dominated speeches and monologues, O'Brien's approach was refreshingly different. He kept the humor light and engaging, ensuring that the focus remained on the achievements of the nominees and the magic of filmmaking. His self-deprecating humor, a trademark of his career, made the audience feel at ease, while his occasional jabs at Hollywood traditions added a touch of irreverence without crossing the line into controversy.

One of the night's standout moments was O'Brien's comedic musical performance, a segment that combined satire and spectacle in a way only he could deliver. Playing off the common criticism that awards shows run too long, he performed a song about not wasting the audience's time. The irony of a musical number addressing efficiency was not lost on the crowd, who laughed and applauded throughout.

Beyond his monologue and scripted bits, O'Brien's interactions with presenters and winners kept the energy of the show high. His experience as a late-night host allowed him to handle unexpected moments with ease. Whether it was playfully teasing nervous winners or smoothly recovering from an onstage technical mishap, his ability to think on his feet was on full display.

The ceremony itself was a grand affair, with the stage at the Dolby Theatre designed to reflect the elegance and prestige of Hollywood. Gold, deep red, and shimmering lights created a regal backdrop, reminding everyone why the Oscars remain the most celebrated night in film. As expected, the biggest awards of the night were met with anticipation, and O'Brien's ability to balance humor with the gravity of the moment ensured that each winner received their due recognition.

OSCARS 2025 HIGHLIGHTS

A highlight of the evening was the historic win for Anora, which took home five awards, including Best Picture. O'Brien's reaction to the unexpected sweep was both hilarious and heartfelt, as he jokingly asked if the film's director had secretly bribed Academy voters. His humor made the moment feel even more special, adding an extra layer of entertainment to the already emotional victories.

While the Oscars are known for their polished presentation, no ceremony is complete without a few surprises. One of the night's most talked-about moments was O'Brien's unexpected onstage exchange with a legendary Hollywood director. In an unplanned twist, the filmmaker playfully interrupted O'Brien's segment to offer his own comedic take on the night's events, leading to an impromptu exchange that had the audience roaring with laughter.

The night also saw a few nods to Hollywood's rich history. A tribute to past Oscar hosts included a montage of iconic moments from legends such as Johnny Carson, Billy Crystal, and Whoopi Goldberg. O'Brien, never one to shy away from a joke at his own expense, humorously noted that his inclusion in the montage might be premature, considering it was only his first time hosting.

Another key feature of the ceremony was its streamlined format. The Academy had been under pressure in recent years to shorten the broadcast, and this year's event was notably efficient. O'Brien played a role in this by keeping segments tight and transitions smooth. His comedic timing helped maintain the pacing, preventing the show from feeling drawn out.

As the ceremony drew to a close, O'Brien's farewell remarks struck the perfect balance between humor and sincerity. He thanked the nominees, the audience, and the Academy for allowing him to host, ending the night on a high note. His final joke—suggesting that he had secretly stashed one of the Oscar statuettes backstage—left the audience laughing as the credits rolled.

Conan O'Brien's hosting of the 97th Academy Awards proved to be one of the most memorable in recent years.

His ability to entertain without overshadowing the winners, his knack for handling surprises with grace, and his undeniable charm made him a standout choice for the role. Whether or not he returns as host in the future, one thing is certain: his performance left an indelible mark on the history of the Oscars.

Presenters and other Highlights

The 97th Academy Awards was a spectacular celebration of the film industry, filled with memorable moments, distinguished presenters, and remarkable performances. Conan O'Brien took center stage as the host, marking his first time leading the prestigious event. His selection came after months of speculation, with reports suggesting that the Academy initially considered a format with multiple hosts. Various names, including Ryan Reynolds and Hugh Jackman, were rumored to be in contention, but ultimately, the choice settled on O'Brien. Known for his sharp wit and extensive experience in television, he brought a unique blend of humor and charm to the ceremony, ensuring the night remained engaging and entertaining from start to finish.

The evening was filled with exciting presentations from some of Hollywood's most beloved figures. Nick Offerman served as the official announcer, guiding the audience through the ceremony and ensuring smooth transitions between segments. The first major award of the night, Best Supporting Actor, was presented by Robert Downey Jr., who added a touch of charisma to the announcement. Best Animated Feature and Best Animated Short Film were introduced by an ensemble that included Andrew Garfield, Goldie Hawn, Lily-Rose Depp, Elle Fanning, John Lithgow, and Connie Nielsen, making it a star-studded moment that highlighted the importance of animation in filmmaking. Bowen Yang followed with the presentation of Best Costume Design, a category that always showcases the creativity and artistic vision behind the films.

Amy Poehler and Scarlett Johansson teamed up to present both Best Original Screenplay and Best Adapted

Screenplay, two awards that honor the writers who bring compelling stories to life. June Squibb then took the stage to announce Best Makeup and Hairstyling, recognizing the work that transforms actors into their on-screen characters. A special tribute segment followed, led by Halle Berry, who honored the recipients of the Governors Awards and introduced a dedicated tribute to Barbara Broccoli and Michael G. Wilson for their contributions to the James Bond franchise. Daryl Hannah presented Best Film Editing, emphasizing the role of seamless storytelling in cinema.

Da'Vine Joy Randolph had the honor of announcing Best Supporting Actress, while Ben Stiller presented Best Production Design, celebrating the intricate set designs that bring cinematic worlds to life. The award for Best Original Song was a standout moment, with Mick Jagger and Selena Gomez taking the stage to present the honor. Samuel L. Jackson and Miley Cyrus paired up to present Best Documentary Short Film and Best Documentary Feature, ensuring that the night also celebrated impactful non-fiction storytelling.

OSCARS 2025 HIGHLIGHTS

Miles Teller and Gal Gadot announced Best Sound, while Rachel Zegler and Ana de Armas took on the responsibility of revealing the winner for Best Visual Effects. Sterling K. Brown followed with the presentation of Best Live Action Short Film. One of the most anticipated segments of the evening was the "In Memoriam" tribute, which honored influential figures in the film industry who had passed away. Morgan Freeman led the heartfelt segment, paying tribute to Gene Hackman and remembering the contributions of legendary figures across the industry.

Other notable presentations included Zoe Saldaña announcing Best Cinematography, Penélope Cruz presenting Best International Feature Film, and Mark Hamill taking the stage to introduce Best Original Score. Whoopi Goldberg and Oprah Winfrey delivered a moving tribute to Quincy Jones, highlighting his enduring impact on the film and music industries. Cillian Murphy announced the winner for Best Actor, and acclaimed filmmaker Quentin Tarantino presented the Best Director award. The prestigious Best Actress award was introduced by Emma Stone, while Billy Crystal and Meg Ryan closed the night with the grand announcement of Best Picture, the most coveted award of the evening.

The ceremony was further elevated by a series of spectacular musical performances. Michael Bearden served as the conductor and musical director, ensuring the event's orchestral arrangements were flawless. Cynthia Erivo and Ariana Grande took the stage for a stunning medley from Wicked, performing songs such as "Over the Rainbow," "Home," and "Defying Gravity." Conan O'Brien himself participated in the entertainment by performing "I Won't Waste Time" during the opening segment, a humorous and self-aware musical number that resonated with the audience.

A special tribute to James Bond featured an electrifying set of performances by Lisa, Doja Cat, and Raye. Lisa delivered a powerful rendition of "Live and Let Die," Doja Cat performed "Diamonds Are Forever," and Raye sang "Skyfall," creating a mesmerizing homage to the iconic franchise. The Los Angeles Master Chorale provided a moving performance of "Lacrimosa" from Mozart's Requiem during the "In Memoriam" segment, adding a solemn and reflective tone to the evening. Queen Latifah brought energy to the tribute for Quincy Jones by performing "Ease on Down the Road," a classic song that perfectly honored his musical legacy.

Behind the scenes, a dedicated team of producers and directors worked tirelessly to ensure the night ran smoothly. In October 2024, the Academy announced that Raj Kapoor and Katy Mullan would return as producers for the second consecutive year, while Hamish Hamilton was selected as the director of the telecast for the fifth time. Academy CEO Bill Kramer and President Janet Yang praised the team for their creativity and passion for filmmaking, highlighting their commitment to delivering an exceptional show. Kapoor and Mullan expressed their excitement in leading the production once again, emphasizing their goal of creating a memorable experience for movie lovers worldwide.

OSCARS 2025 HIGHLIGHTS

Several changes were implemented for this year's ceremony. The Academy announced that past winners would not present the acting awards, moving away from the "Fab 5" format that had been reintroduced the previous year. Instead, notable Oscar winners were invited to highlight the contributions of behind-the-scenes talent in other categories. This year's event also featured a special tribute to James Bond producers Barbara Broccoli and Michael G. Wilson, who were honored with the Irving G. Thalberg Memorial Award.

For the third consecutive year, a dedicated segment celebrated the impact of the James Bond franchise. Additionally, Amelia Dimoldenberg returned as the social media ambassador and red carpet correspondent, bringing a fresh and engaging presence to the pre-show coverage. For the first time in history, the Oscars were streamed live on Hulu and internationally on Disney+, expanding the ceremony's reach to a global audience. ABC also announced a special post-Oscars preview of American Idol Season 23, ensuring that viewers remained engaged even after the final award was presented.

The event was not without its challenges. Leading up to the ceremony, devastating wildfires in Southern California disrupted the usual preparations. Voting deadlines for Academy members had to be extended, and the nominations announcement was delayed due to the crisis. In response, the Academy made several adjustments to honor the Los Angeles community's resilience and contributions to the film industry. One significant change was the decision not to feature live performances of the Best Original Song nominees. Instead, the songwriters were showcased through personal reflections and behind-the-scenes footage. This decision sparked controversy, with industry professionals arguing that it diminished the importance of music in film. Diane Warren, a nominee for "The Journey" from The Six Triple Eight, publicly criticized the move, calling it unfair to both the nominees and the audience.

Conan O'Brien acknowledged the difficulties posed by the wildfires and expressed his commitment to handling the hosting duties with sensitivity. In an interview, he emphasized the importance of approaching the situation with humility, acknowledging the tragedies affecting the community. He and his writing team worked to strike a balance between humor and respect, ensuring that the evening remained celebratory without ignoring the challenges that shaped the event's backdrop.

Despite careful planning, technical difficulties arose during the ceremony. Hulu, which was streaming the event live, experienced multiple crashes, frustrating viewers and causing interruptions in the broadcast. The most significant failure occurred just before the Best Actress award was announced, cutting the live stream short for many audiences. This issue led to widespread criticism, with many calling for improvements in the streaming service's infrastructure for future live events.

Best Picture Winner and Its Impact

The 97th Academy Awards proved to be a night of surprises, celebrations, and history-making moments, but nothing defined the event more than the victory of Anora as Best Picture. The film, directed by Sean Baker, stood out in a competitive field that included major contenders like The Brutalist, Emilia Pérez, Wicked, and Dune: Part Two. While the race for Best Picture was one of the most unpredictable in recent years, Anora emerged victorious, marking a significant moment for independent cinema and reinforcing the Academy's recognition of bold storytelling.

From the moment the nominations were announced, Anora was seen as an underdog. With six nominations, it was up against films with larger budgets, widespread global appeal, and more traditional Oscar pedigrees. Yet, Anora had one thing that set it apart—its originality. The film was widely praised for its fresh perspective, strong performances, and Sean Baker's unique directorial style. The movie's success at Cannes had already generated significant buzz, and its comparisons to the works of the Coen Brothers and Quentin Tarantino helped it gain a loyal following among both critics and Academy voters.

The Best Picture win for Anora was more than just a trophy; it was a statement. Hollywood has long been dominated by big-budget productions and films backed by major studios. Yet, in recent years, there has been a noticeable shift toward recognizing smaller, independent films that bring something different to the table. Anora winning over blockbusters like Dune: Part Two and Wicked signaled the Academy's continued appreciation for intimate storytelling that connects with audiences on a personal level.

One of the biggest reasons Anora made such an impact was its director, Sean Baker. Known for his ability to capture raw, authentic stories about everyday people, Baker had already established himself with films like The Florida Project and Tangerine. His approach to filmmaking often includes working with unknown actors and shooting on location to bring a sense of realism to his work. Anora was no exception. The film's lead actress, Mikey Madison, delivered a performance that earned her the Best Actress award, further solidifying Anora as one of the defining films of the year.

The story of Anora follows a young woman navigating a world filled with difficult choices, unexpected circumstances, and moments of personal growth. It is a film that resonates with many viewers because of its relatability and emotional depth. Unlike some of the other contenders, which relied on elaborate production designs, visual effects, or historical narratives, Anora thrived on its simplicity. This made it stand out in a way that felt refreshing, proving that a film does not need an enormous budget to tell a powerful story.

The impact of Anora's win goes beyond just the Oscar itself. Independent filmmakers everywhere now have another example of how unique storytelling can triumph in an industry often driven by commercial success. The film's victory sends a message to studios, investors, and aspiring directors that audiences are still drawn to well-crafted narratives that feel real and meaningful. It also reaffirms that the Academy is willing to step outside the expected formula for Best Picture winners, rewarding creativity over spectacle.

Another major takeaway from Anora's success is the influence of the preferential ballot system used in Oscar voting. Unlike a simple majority vote, the Best Picture category is decided by a ranked-choice system. This means that a film does not necessarily need to be everyone's first choice to win—it just needs to be widely liked across the board. Many industry experts believe that Anora benefited from this system because it was a film that many voters appreciated, even if it was not their top choice. Its broad appeal allowed it to gain enough second and third-place votes to surpass more polarizing films like Emilia Pérez and The Brutalist.

While Anora celebrated its well-deserved victory, the film industry also took notice of how its win reflects broader trends. Over the past decade, Oscar winners have shifted from large-scale epics to more intimate, character-driven films. From Moonlight to Nomadland, the Academy has increasingly favored stories that focus on human experiences rather than grand spectacle. Anora fits perfectly into this trend, demonstrating that films with smaller budgets and unconventional narratives can compete at the highest level.

The film's success also highlights the evolving nature of independent cinema. Streaming services, digital distribution, and social media have made it easier for smaller films to reach wider audiences. Anora had a strong presence on the festival circuit and relied on word-of-mouth marketing, which helped it gain momentum leading up to the Oscars. Its triumph shows that with the right combination of strong storytelling, dedicated performances, and smart marketing, independent films can stand alongside major studio productions.

Another aspect of Anora's win that cannot be ignored is its impact on actors and filmmakers looking for their big break. Hollywood has long been a place where opportunities are often given to those with connections, but Anora serves as a reminder that talent and hard work can lead to recognition, regardless of background. Mikey Madison's Best Actress win is particularly significant, as she was not a household name before this film. Her performance captivated audiences and critics alike, proving that new faces in the industry can rise to the top with the right role.

Of course, Anora's success does not mean that big-budget films are losing their place at the Oscars. Dune: Part Two still managed to take home awards in technical categories, while Wicked won for its production design and costume design. These wins show that there is still a place for large-scale filmmaking in Hollywood, but they also suggest that audiences and voters are looking for a balance between spectacle and substance.

The influence of Anora's victory will likely be felt for years to come. Its win could encourage studios to take more risks on smaller films, knowing that they have the potential to succeed both critically and commercially. It may also inspire more filmmakers to tell bold, unconventional stories without worrying about whether their film fits the traditional mold of an Oscar-winning movie.

The impact of Anora extends beyond the Oscars. Independent filmmakers now have a renewed sense of hope that their work can be recognized at the highest level. Studios may start investing in more diverse stories and filmmakers who bring fresh perspectives to the screen. The industry as a whole may continue shifting toward rewarding originality over formulaic storytelling.

About Anora

The reception of Anora at the box office and among critics reflected its strong impact on audiences worldwide. By February 26, 2025, the film had earned $15.7 million in the United States and Canada, with an additional $25.2 million from international markets, bringing its total earnings to

$40.9 million. The movie had an impressive start, debuting in just six theaters and making $550,503 during its opening weekend. Its per-screen average of $91,751 was the highest of 2024, surpassing Kinds of Kindness, and ranked second overall since the COVID-19 pandemic, following Asteroid City. As Anora expanded its release, it continued performing well, earning $908,830 in its second weekend across 34 theaters and later making $1.8 million from 253 locations. By its fourth weekend, the film had reached 1,104 theaters, where it grossed $2.5 million.

Critically, Anora received overwhelming praise. On Rotten Tomatoes, 93% of 332 critics gave it a positive rating, with an average score of 8.5/10. The site's consensus described the film as another outstanding example of Sean Baker's talent for capturing the struggles of everyday Americans, with Mikey Madison's bold performance adding an extra layer of depth. Metacritic also reflected this positive response, giving the film a score of 91 out of 100, signifying widespread acclaim based on 62 reviews. In France, AlloCiné reported an average rating of 4.2 out of 5 from 45 critics, further demonstrating its global appeal.

OSCARS 2025 HIGHLIGHTS

Greta Gerwig, president of the 77th Cannes Film Festival Jury, spoke highly of the film, stating that the jury was deeply moved by its storytelling. She noted that Anora felt both innovative and in dialogue with classic cinema, comparing its style to the works of Ernst Lubitsch and Howard Hawks while maintaining a fresh and unpredictable approach.

Mikey Madison's portrayal of the lead character earned her the Academy Award for Best Actress. Reviews singled out her performance as a highlight of the film. Richard Lawson of Vanity Fair described Anora as an audacious and energetic experience. He acknowledged that while some moments in Baker's storytelling felt repetitive, Madison's performance kept the film engaging. He also pointed out that Baker's depiction of outsiders often fluctuates between empathy and detachment. Justin Chang of The New Yorker compared the film to a whirlwind dream, shifting between joy and disaster with an unpredictable flow. He saw Anora as a contemporary twist on classic screwball comedies, filled with both humor and sharp social commentary.

The film earned recognition from major publications, with Sight and Sound ranking it as the second-best film of 2024, while Film Comment included it in its top ten list. In 2025, Collider placed Anora at number 36 in its ranking of the best movies of the decade, with Jeremy Urquhart describing it as a modern classic. Several filmmakers and actors praised the film, but some discussions around its themes led to controversy.

One of the most debated aspects of Anora was its reception in Russia. Due to its story involving a Russian oligarch's son, some Russian audiences viewed its Oscar nominations as a point of national pride. Screenwriter Mikhail Idov, known for his work in Russian cinema, wrote in The New York Times that while he admired the film, he found it unsettling that it was being celebrated in Russia, especially given the country's ongoing geopolitical conflicts.

The film's portrayal of sex work also sparked discussions. Many sex workers praised Anora for presenting a more nuanced depiction of their profession compared to past films, which often treated it as either a tragedy or a moral failing. Writing for Slate, Risdon Roberts compared Anora's protagonist to Vivian Ward from Pretty Woman, noting that unlike past depictions, Ani was not portrayed as a helpless victim or someone in need of saving. Instead, the film established her as sharp, skilled, and fully in control of her choices. The opening credits scene, where Ani confidently works the floor of an upscale strip club, immediately positioned her as a capable and intelligent character rather than a stereotype.

Tiff Smith highlighted how Anora presented sex work as just one aspect of Ani's life, rather than defining her entire existence. This, according to Smith, is what true representation looks like—showing characters as fully developed individuals rather than reducing them to their profession. Others commended Baker's decision to hire sex workers as consultants and cast members, which contributed to the film's authenticity, particularly in its depiction of the daily realities of working in a strip club.

However, not all reactions were positive. Some critics argued that the film relied on outdated stereotypes about sex workers being vulnerable and in need of rescue. A UK-based sex worker criticized Anora for reinforcing the idea of the "traumatized, fragile sex worker" trope that has been seen repeatedly in cinema. Marla Cruz noted that while the film was engaging, it failed to explore Ani's life outside of her profession. She argued that there was little insight into the distinction between Ani as a person and Ani as a worker, which could have added more depth to her character.

Film scholar Ayanna Dozier also weighed in, stating that Anora continued the tradition of depicting sex workers as projections of society's fantasies rather than fully realized individuals. While the film challenged some clichés, it still presented Ani's story in a way that left room for debate about how much agency she truly had. Cruz further questioned whether Ani's character evolved over the course of the film or if she remained trapped in the same cycle of power struggles with the men around her.

While many viewers found the film's ending satisfying, others criticized it for leaning too heavily on romanticized notions of rescue. Roberts, while largely positive about the film, pointed out that for real-life sex workers, financial independence and safety are far more pressing concerns than finding a man to change their circumstances. She wrote that rather than positioning clients as saviors, the film should have leaned further into the reality that, for many, sex work is a calculated means to an end rather than a source of emotional fulfillment.

Despite these debates, Anora left a lasting impression on audiences and critics alike. The film's commercial success, critical acclaim, and recognition at major film festivals cemented its status as one of the most talked-about films of the year. Whether viewed as a groundbreaking portrayal of modern struggles or a film that still carried lingering stereotypes, it sparked conversations that extended far beyond the theater. The discussions surrounding Anora highlight the evolving ways in which cinema portrays sex work, gender dynamics, and power, ensuring that the film's impact will be felt for years to come.

Outstanding Directing Achievement

Sean Baker's victory at the 97th Academy Awards was a defining moment in filmmaking. Winning the Best Director award for Anora, he proved that independent cinema still has the power to compete with big-budget productions. His work stood out in a competitive year, earning him recognition not just as a director but as a filmmaker who can tell raw and powerful stories without the backing of major studios. His ability to balance humor with deep social commentary made Anora a film that resonated with audiences and critics alike.

Baker's career has always been about capturing real-life struggles in an honest and engaging way. His films focus on people who often go unnoticed by mainstream Hollywood. Whether it's sex workers, immigrants, or those living on the fringes of society, Baker has consistently highlighted their lives with authenticity. His early films, including Tangerine and The Florida Project, established him as a director who could take unconventional subjects and turn them into deeply human stories. With Anora, he continued this tradition, bringing his signature style to a broader audience.

The success of Anora did not come as a surprise to those who have followed Baker's work. The film had already won major awards leading up to the Oscars, including the Palme d'Or at Cannes and Best Picture at the Critics' Choice Awards. Still, the competition at the Academy Awards was fierce. He was up against accomplished directors such as Brady Corbet (The Brutalist), James Mangold (A Complete Unknown), Jacques Audiard (Emilia Pérez), and Coralie Fargeat (The Substance). Each of these directors had created films that were strong contenders for the award, but Baker's work stood out because of its originality, strong storytelling, and ability to connect with viewers on a personal level.

When Baker stepped on stage to accept the Best Director award, he used his speech to emphasize the importance of keeping cinema alive. He spoke about how the film industry is changing, with streaming services dominating the market and traditional theater-going experiences becoming less common. He urged filmmakers to continue making films for the big screen, stressing that watching a movie in a theater is a communal experience that cannot be replaced by home viewing. His words resonated with many in the audience, reminding everyone why cinema has always been a powerful form of storytelling.

What makes Baker's achievement even more remarkable is that he did not just direct Anora—he wrote, produced, and edited it as well. This level of involvement is rare in Hollywood, where most directors rely on teams of writers and editors to bring their vision to life. Baker's hands-on approach allowed him to maintain full creative control over the project, ensuring that every aspect of the film reflected his artistic vision. His win also made history, as he became the first person to win four Oscars for a single film, tying Walt Disney's record for the most Academy Awards won in a single night.

Baker's rise in the film industry has been anything but conventional. Born in Summit, New Jersey, he developed a love for movies at a young age. Unlike many directors who start with big-budget productions, Baker began his career with micro-budget films that focused on real-life stories. His breakthrough came with Tangerine, a film shot entirely on an iPhone, which demonstrated his ability to create compelling narratives even with limited resources. The Florida Project further cemented his reputation, earning critical acclaim for its portrayal of a struggling mother and her daughter living in a motel near Disney World. These films showcased Baker's talent for blending humor with deep emotional storytelling, a skill that he perfected with Anora.

The story of Anora follows a Brooklyn exotic dancer who unexpectedly marries the son of a Russian oligarch during a drug-fueled trip to Las Vegas. What starts as a whirlwind romance quickly turns chaotic when the groom's wealthy parents send their henchmen to force an annulment. The film masterfully blends comedy with a sharp critique of wealth, power, and the unpredictability of life. Mikey

Madison's lead performance was widely praised, and she went on to win the Best Actress award, further solidifying Anora as one of the standout films of the year.

One of the reasons Anora resonated with so many people was Baker's ability to tell a story that felt both outrageous and deeply human. The characters were flawed, relatable, and unpredictable, making them feel real despite the film's exaggerated circumstances. Baker's directing style, which often involves working with non-professional actors and capturing scenes in real-world locations, added to the authenticity of the film. His dedication to telling stories about marginalized groups was evident once again, as Anora explored themes of class differences, personal ambition, and the unpredictable nature of love and money.

Baker has often spoken about the struggles of independent filmmakers in an industry that increasingly favors large-scale productions. He has voiced concerns that indie films are becoming nothing more than stepping stones for directors who eventually move on to studio projects. For Baker, independent filmmaking is not just a phase—it is a commitment to telling stories that mainstream Hollywood often ignores. His success with Anora is proof that audiences still crave original storytelling that doesn't rely on CGI, explosions, or franchise connections.

Winning Best Director at the Oscars is a career-defining moment for any filmmaker, but for Baker, it is also an opportunity to advocate for change in the industry. He hopes that his win will inspire studios and investors to take more risks on independent projects, proving that films with smaller budgets can be just as impactful as their blockbuster counterparts. His win also sends a message to aspiring directors that they do not need millions of dollars to create something meaningful. What matters is a strong story, a unique perspective, and the ability to connect with audiences.

The 97th Academy Awards highlighted the growing appreciation for directors who bring their own vision to life. This year's nominees in the Best Director category were all first-time contenders, a rare occurrence that reflected the Academy's evolving recognition of new voices in filmmaking. Baker's win over seasoned directors like James Mangold and Jacques Audiard further demonstrated that originality and creativity are being valued more than ever.

Baker has already hinted that his next project will continue his exploration of untold stories. He remains dedicated to shedding light on the lives of those often overlooked by Hollywood, and his success with Anora will likely give him even more freedom to pursue bold and unconventional ideas. His career has shown that filmmaking is not just about budgets and box office numbers—it is about storytelling, creativity, and the ability to make audiences feel something real.

Notable Acting Awards

The 97th Academy Awards honored outstanding achievements in film, with the acting categories receiving significant attention. These awards recognized exceptional performances that captivated audiences and showcased the depth of talent in the industry. This year's winners delivered unforgettable portrayals, earning their place among the most celebrated actors in cinema.

Adrien Brody won Best Actor for his performance in The Brutalist, portraying architect László Tóth. The film follows Tóth's journey through personal and professional struggles, exploring themes of ambition, loss, and resilience. Brody's portrayal was widely praised for its depth and intensity. He is known for his commitment to his roles, often immersing himself completely in the character's world. His performance in The Brutalist was no exception, capturing the internal conflicts of a man burdened by his past while striving to leave a lasting impact through his work. His ability to convey emotion through subtle expressions and body language made his portrayal compelling. Brody had previously won an Oscar for The Pianist, and his latest victory reaffirmed his reputation as one of the most dedicated actors in Hollywood. His acceptance speech reflected his deep connection to the role, expressing gratitude for the opportunity to bring such a powerful character to life.

Mikey Madison won Best Actress for her role in Anora, a film that explores the life of a young woman caught in a whirlwind of love, ambition, and adversity. Madison's portrayal was praised for its realism, emotional depth, and authenticity. Her character navigates a complex world, facing difficult choices and personal challenges. Madison's ability to convey vulnerability while maintaining a strong presence on screen set her performance apart. This win marked a major milestone in her career, solidifying her status as a leading actress. During her acceptance speech, she thanked director Sean Baker for his vision and dedication to storytelling. She also highlighted the importance of independent cinema and how it allows for bold, unconventional narratives to be told. Her speech resonated with many in the industry, as it emphasized the impact of films that challenge traditional storytelling norms.

Kieran Culkin won Best Actor for A Real Pain, a film that blended humor with deep emotional themes. Culkin's performance showcased his ability to balance lighthearted moments with intense, introspective scenes. He brought a unique charm to the role, making his character relatable and engaging. Having built a strong reputation in television, this victory marked a significant transition for him into leading film roles. His acceptance speech was filled with gratitude, acknowledging the team that made the film possible. He spoke about how the project allowed him to push his limits as an actor and explore new aspects of his craft. His win was widely celebrated, as he had been a favorite throughout the awards season.

Zoe Saldaña won Best Actress for Emilia Pérez, a film that explored themes of justice, identity, and redemption. Her portrayal was a departure from the roles she had been known for, showcasing her ability to take on dramatically different characters. Saldaña's performance was both powerful and deeply moving, bringing a new level of recognition to her talent. Her ability to convey complex emotions while maintaining a commanding presence on screen made her performance stand out. She dedicated her award to her fellow cast members and the film's director, expressing appreciation for the opportunity to work on a project that told such an important story. Her win was also a moment of recognition for films that challenge conventions and push the boundaries of traditional storytelling.

The acting categories at the 97th Academy Awards were notable not only for the individual performances but also for the broader impact of the films themselves. Many of the winning films tackled complex social themes, bringing attention to issues that resonate with audiences. Anora, which won multiple awards, was a prime example of a film that used storytelling to challenge perceptions and spark meaningful conversations. The film's success highlighted the growing influence of independent cinema and the ability of smaller films to compete at the highest level.

The night also marked a historic moment with the nomination of Karla Sofía Gascón for her performance in Emilia Pérez. She became the first transgender actress to be nominated in a lead acting category, a milestone that underscored the evolving landscape of the film industry. Her nomination was widely celebrated as a step forward for representation and inclusivity in cinema. Although she did not win, her presence in the category was a significant achievement that highlighted the importance of diverse voices in storytelling.

Sean Baker, the director of Anora, was another major winner of the night. His film dominated multiple categories, reinforcing his reputation as a visionary filmmaker. His dedication to authentic storytelling and his ability to capture raw, unfiltered performances contributed to the film's success. His work exemplified how independent films can leave a lasting impact, challenging mainstream cinema while gaining critical acclaim. His wins were seen as a victory not just for him but for independent filmmakers striving to bring unique stories to the screen.

Adrien Brody's win was a reminder of how an actor's dedication to a role can elevate a film to new heights. His ability to transform into his character made The Brutalist an unforgettable experience for audiences. His performance was not just about delivering lines but about fully inhabiting the world of his character. Every gesture, every pause, and every expression added depth to his portrayal, making it one of the most talked-about performances of the year.

Mikey Madison's victory was significant because it signaled a new era for young actresses who are willing to take on challenging roles. Her portrayal in Anora demonstrated her range, proving that she could carry a film with emotional depth and authenticity. Her ability to connect with audiences on a personal level made her performance stand out, and her win was a testament to the power of raw, unfiltered storytelling.

Kieran Culkin's performance in A Real Pain resonated with audiences because of its relatability. His character's journey was filled with moments of humor and introspection, creating a performance that felt both natural and deeply affecting. His ability to shift between comedic and dramatic moments showcased his versatility as an actor. His win was a defining moment in his career, opening new doors for him in the film industry.

Zoe Saldaña's victory was another highlight of the night, as it recognized her ability to take on a deeply emotional role and deliver a performance that felt both powerful and authentic. Her work in Emilia Pérez allowed her to explore new dimensions of acting, moving beyond her previous roles and proving that she could excel in dramatic cinema. Her win was a celebration of her growth as an actress and her willingness to take on challenging material.

The 97th Academy Awards not only recognized outstanding performances but also reflected the changing landscape of the film industry. The acting categories were filled with performances that pushed boundaries and brought new perspectives to the screen. The success of Anora, The Brutalist, and Emilia Pérez demonstrated how films that focus on storytelling and character depth can resonate with audiences and critics alike. The night was a celebration of talent, dedication, and the power of film to inspire and challenge perceptions.

Recognizing Supporting Performances

The 97th Academy Awards celebrated outstanding achievements in film, with supporting performances playing a crucial role in some of the most memorable moments of the night. While lead actors often receive the most attention, supporting performances bring depth, nuance, and emotional weight to a film. They enhance the story, create compelling dynamics with the main characters, and often steal the show with their powerful presence. This year's winners in the supporting categories exemplified the importance of these roles, delivering performances that left a lasting impact on audiences and critics alike.

Kieran Culkin won the Oscar for Best Supporting Actor for A Real Pain. His performance stood out for its ability to balance humor and raw emotion. Culkin's character brought both lightheartedness and depth to the film, making his presence on screen both entertaining and meaningful. Throughout his career, Culkin has been known for his impeccable comedic timing and ability to portray deeply flawed yet relatable characters. His role in A Real Pain allowed him to showcase both sides of his talent. The film's unique tone—a blend of comedy and introspection—was elevated by his performance, making his win well-deserved. His acceptance speech reflected his gratitude for being part of a project that allowed him to explore new dimensions of acting. Culkin's win was significant, as it marked a turning point in his career, solidifying his transition from television to film in a major way.

Zoe Saldaña took home the Oscar for Best Supporting Actress for her performance in Emilia Pérez. Known for her work in action and sci-fi blockbusters, Saldaña took on a dramatically different role in this film, showcasing a depth of emotion that critics praised. Emilia Pérez was a film that challenged traditional storytelling, and Saldaña's role was essential in bringing its themes to life. Her character required a delicate balance between strength and vulnerability, and she delivered a performance that resonated deeply. Winning this award was a defining moment in her career, proving her ability to tackle complex roles beyond the action-packed franchises she had become associated with. Her speech was heartfelt, as she acknowledged the importance of diverse storytelling and the impact of her role on her own perspective as an actress.

Supporting performances often provide the foundation for a film's emotional core. While lead roles drive the central narrative, supporting actors add richness to the story, creating memorable interactions and helping to develop the lead characters. This year's winners embodied this idea, making their films stronger through their presence. Their performances were a reminder that great storytelling is not just about the main character but also about the world that surrounds them.

Beyond the winners, the supporting categories featured strong contenders who delivered exceptional performances. In the Best Supporting Actress category, Monica Barbaro (A Complete Unknown), Ariana Grande (Wicked), Felicity Jones (The Brutalist), and Isabella

Rossellini (Conclave) all played key roles in bringing their films to life. Each of these actresses contributed something unique, elevating their respective stories through their performances. Their portrayals added emotional weight, humor, or dramatic tension, proving that supporting roles are often just as essential as lead performances.

In the Best Supporting Actor category, the competition was equally fierce. Yura Borisov (Anora), Edward Norton (A Complete Unknown), Guy Pearce (The Brutalist), and Jeremy Strong (The Apprentice) delivered performances that left a strong impression on audiences. Each of these actors played a crucial role in shaping their film's narrative, providing moments of intensity, humor, or emotional resonance that strengthened the overall story.

One of the most remarkable aspects of this year's awards was the way supporting performances helped to challenge traditional storytelling. Emilia Pérez, in particular, was praised for its innovative approach, and Saldaña's performance played a crucial role in making its unconventional narrative work. Her character served as an anchor in the film's complex story, making the emotional beats even more impactful. Her win highlighted the importance of taking risks in acting and how supporting performances can be just as transformative as leading roles.

Kieran Culkin's performance in A Real Pain was another example of how a supporting role can shape the tone and emotional depth of a film. His ability to bring humor to serious moments without diminishing their impact made his character essential to the film's success. His dynamic with the lead actors created a compelling relationship that made the film's themes more relatable and engaging. His win was a recognition of his skill in blending comedy and drama seamlessly.

The acknowledgment of these performances also spoke to a broader trend in Hollywood—one that values nuanced, character-driven storytelling. Films like Emilia Pérez and A Real Pain demonstrated that audiences appreciate stories with depth, where every character serves a purpose. The recognition of these supporting performances showed an appreciation for actors who bring authenticity to their roles, even when they are not in the spotlight.

Supporting roles often allow actors to take creative risks, and this year's winners exemplified that idea. Saldaña's willingness to step outside her usual genre and embrace a challenging, emotionally layered role paid off in a big way. Similarly, Culkin's ability to bring humor and sincerity to his performance helped create one of the most memorable characters of the year. These wins were not just personal victories for the actors but also a win for storytelling that values depth and complexity.

The celebration of supporting performances at the Academy Awards also highlighted the importance of collaboration in filmmaking. While lead actors may carry the primary storyline, it is often the supporting cast that gives a film its richness. Great films are not just about one standout performance; they are about a collection of performances that work together to create something meaningful. Saldaña and Culkin's wins were a testament to the power of ensemble storytelling, where every role, no matter its size, contributes to the film's impact.

These awards also served as a reminder that supporting performances can sometimes outshine leading roles. Many iconic moments in film history have come from supporting actors who delivered unforgettable lines, scenes, or emotional beats. This year's winners continued that tradition, proving that supporting roles are just as vital to a film's success as the leads.

As the awards season came to a close, the recognition of these supporting performances reinforced the idea that great acting is about more than just screen time. It is about making a lasting impression, bringing depth to a character, and elevating the story as a whole. Saldaña and Culkin's victories were a celebration of the art of acting in all its forms, showing that every performance, no matter its size, has the potential to be truly remarkable.

Technical and Artistic Excellence

The 97th Academy Awards celebrated technical and artistic excellence across various categories, highlighting the dedication, craftsmanship, and creativity that go into filmmaking. This year's winners demonstrated an extraordinary level of precision, innovation, and emotional depth, proving that great cinema is not just about storytelling but also about the technical and artistic elements that bring those stories to life. From cinematography to production design, from original score to visual effects, each award honored the incredible efforts of individuals and teams who transformed scripts into breathtaking visual and auditory experiences.

One of the standout winners of the night was The Brutalist, which took home multiple awards, including Best Cinematography. Cinematographer Lol Crawley's work in the film was widely praised for its striking visual compositions, lighting techniques, and immersive framing. The film, shot on VistaVision, a format not used by an American movie since 1961, created a unique visual language that set it apart. Crawley's approach to cinematography played a crucial role in bringing the world of The Brutalist to life, emphasizing the film's architectural themes and the emotional weight of its protagonist's journey. His win was a recognition of the meticulous planning and execution that went into crafting each frame, proving that cinematography is more than just capturing images—it is about shaping the emotional tone of a film.

Another major technical achievement came in the form of Best Original Score, which was awarded to Daniel Blumberg for The Brutalist. The music in the film was more than just background sound; it was an essential part of the storytelling, heightening the tension, evoking deep emotions, and complementing the film's visuals. Blumberg's acceptance speech acknowledged the talented musicians who contributed to the film's score, emphasizing the collaborative nature of composing for film. His work demonstrated how music can transform a movie, reinforcing its themes and enhancing the audience's connection to the story.

Production design was another category that highlighted artistic excellence, with Wicked winning the award for Best Production Design. The film's world-building was a major achievement, transporting audiences into an otherworldly realm filled with intricate details, stunning set pieces, and imaginative environments. Production design is an often-underappreciated aspect of filmmaking, yet it plays a vital role in creating the visual identity of a movie. The team behind Wicked demonstrated an exceptional ability to merge fantasy with reality, ensuring that every element of the set contributed to the film's magical atmosphere. Their win underscored the importance of design in shaping the audience's cinematic experience.

Visual effects were another crucial aspect of this year's awards, with Dune: Part Two taking home the Oscar for Best Visual Effects. The film's seamless integration of CGI and practical effects created a universe that felt both grand and realistic. The visual effects team worked tirelessly to bring Denis Villeneuve's vision to life, ensuring that every frame was visually stunning and technically flawless. Their work extended beyond creating large-scale spectacle; it also played a key role in the film's storytelling, allowing audiences to fully immerse themselves in its futuristic world. The award for Dune: Part Two was a testament to the evolving capabilities of visual effects artists and their ability to push the boundaries of cinematic realism.

Best Sound was another category where Dune: Part Two emerged victorious. Sound design is an essential yet often overlooked component of filmmaking, responsible for creating an auditory landscape that complements the visuals. In Dune: Part Two, the sound team crafted an intricate blend of ambient noise, dialogue, and musical elements that enhanced the film's immersive quality. Whether it was the eerie silence of the desert, the deep resonance of the film's massive sandworms, or the tension-building score, every element of sound was carefully designed to amplify the audience's emotional engagement. This award was a well-deserved recognition of the effort and skill required to create a soundscape that brings a film to life.

Another film that showcased technical and artistic brilliance was The Substance, which won Best Makeup and Hairstyling. The transformative work of the makeup team played a crucial role in shaping the film's narrative, creating characters that felt authentic and visually striking. Makeup and hairstyling are often key in defining a character's identity and evolution throughout a film, and the team behind The Substance executed this with remarkable precision. Their win highlighted how attention to detail in makeup can enhance storytelling, bringing characters to life in ways that deepen the audience's connection to them.

Best Costume Design went to Wicked, a film that required elaborate and imaginative wardrobe choices to bring its fantasy world to life. Costumes are an integral part of storytelling, helping define a film's characters, setting, and mood. Paul Tazewell's designs in Wicked contributed significantly to the film's overall visual spectacle, reinforcing the personalities of the characters while maintaining the grand, theatrical style that fans of the musical would expect. The level of craftsmanship involved in designing these costumes demonstrated how fashion in film is an art form in itself, worthy of recognition and appreciation.

The Oscar for Best Film Editing went to Anora, a film that required precise cutting techniques to maintain its pacing and narrative structure. Editing is a critical component of storytelling, determining how scenes flow together, how tension is built, and how audiences perceive the rhythm of a film. Sean Baker, who not only directed but also edited Anora, displayed a mastery of pacing that allowed the film's emotional beats to land with maximum impact. His win was significant, highlighting how independent films can compete at the highest level when it comes to technical execution.

International and Documentary Recognition

The 97th Academy Awards stood out not only for its celebration of cinematic excellence but also for the powerful statements made on stage. While the independent film Anora swept multiple major categories, it was the win of No Other Land for Best Documentary Feature that sparked some of the night's most intense discussions. This documentary, directed by Basel Adra, Hamdan Ballal, Yuval Abraham, and Rachel Szor, shed light on the realities faced by Palestinians in the occupied West Bank, particularly in Masafer Yatta. The film documented the destruction of Palestinian villages, the struggles of those facing displacement, and the growing—though complicated—relationship between its Israeli and Palestinian filmmakers.

When the directors accepted their award, they chose to use their time on stage to bring attention to the ongoing violence and forced evictions in Palestinian territories rather than focusing on their own journey in making the film. One of the filmmakers, a Palestinian, spoke about his personal fears, particularly after recently becoming a father. He shared his hope that his child would not have to endure the same daily fears of home demolitions and violence that had become normal for his community. His words struck a nerve with many in the audience, while also provoking a divided response from those who viewed the speech through a political lens.

Another director, an Israeli journalist, emphasized the fundamental inequality between himself and his Palestinian co-director. While one lived under civilian law, the other was subjected to a system of military rule that controlled nearly every aspect of his life. The speech was both a call for awareness and a direct challenge to American foreign policy, arguing that the ongoing support of the occupation was a major factor in perpetuating the cycle of suffering. The audience reaction was mixed, with some responding with applause and others expressing discomfort at the bluntness of the message.

Despite its international success, No Other Land struggled to find a major distributor in the United States, a challenge that the filmmakers attributed to the film's political subject matter. To qualify for the Academy Awards, they had to arrange a limited screening in New York. However, despite the lack of widespread theatrical release, the documentary had already gained significant traction, with independent screenings selling out across the country. Its Oscar win further cemented its impact, bringing attention to a topic that mainstream media outlets often approached with caution.

While No Other Land was one of the most politically charged winners of the night, the theme of marginalized communities gaining visibility extended across multiple categories. Anora, the indie film that dominated the ceremony with five wins, brought attention to the lives of sex workers, a group often misrepresented in mainstream media. The film followed the story of a Russian-American stripper living in Brooklyn, navigating a world that offered little stability or security. When an unexpected romance with the son of a wealthy Russian oligarch presented her with the possibility of a different life, she found herself facing both opportunity and devastation.

The film's director, known for creating narratives about those on the fringes of society, used his acceptance speech to acknowledge the real-life sex workers who had shared their stories and experiences to help bring authenticity to the project. His words underscored the importance of portraying these communities with honesty rather than reinforcing harmful stereotypes. The lead actress echoed this sentiment, expressing gratitude to the women she had met while preparing for her role and pledging continued support for sex worker advocacy.

The ceremony also included moments that reinforced the role of cinema in confronting historical injustices. One of the winning international films focused on Brazil's past dictatorship, telling the story of a woman who dedicated her life to uncovering the truth about her husband's disappearance at the hands of the military regime. The film's director paid tribute to her courage and resilience, emphasizing that stories like hers should never be forgotten.

Elsewhere in the night, conversations about democracy, discrimination, and human rights took center stage. A veteran actor who won Best Actor reflected on how his most acclaimed roles had both centered around stories of war, oppression, and anti-Semitism. He spoke about the responsibility of artists to use their platform to highlight the dangers of hate and division, stressing that history had repeatedly shown the devastating consequences of unchecked discrimination. His speech resonated with many, serving as a reminder of the power that film holds in shaping public consciousness.

Diversity and representation also played a significant role in this year's Oscars, with several historic firsts occurring during the ceremony. A costume designer became the first Black man to win in his category, receiving recognition for his work on a major musical adaptation. Overwhelmed with emotion, he acknowledged how significant the moment was, not just for himself but for future generations of designers of color. The audience responded with a standing ovation, marking one of the most uplifting moments of the night.

Another major win came from a Latina actress who became the first American of Dominican descent to take home an Oscar. In her speech, she honored her immigrant family, recalling how her grandmother had arrived in the United States decades earlier with hopes of building a better life. She spoke about the importance of seeing people like herself represented in major films, particularly in roles that allowed her to embrace her cultural identity. Her win was not just a personal triumph but a step forward in breaking barriers for Latina actresses in Hollywood.

While the Oscars are traditionally a night of glamour and celebration, this year's ceremony did not shy away from the harsh realities facing the film industry itself. The struggle of movie theaters to recover from the impact of the pandemic was a recurring topic among winners, with multiple filmmakers using their speeches to encourage audiences to support theaters. The director of Anora emphasized the importance of watching films in a communal setting, describing the unique experience of laughing, crying, and reacting together with a live audience. His remarks were a reminder of the challenges theaters continue to face, especially as streaming services dominate the industry.

Another winner, a veteran actor, spoke candidly about the instability of the profession. While many perceive acting as a glamorous career, he reflected on the unpredictability of success, noting that even those who have reached the highest levels of acclaim can struggle to find work. His words served as a reminder of the difficulties faced by artists at all levels, highlighting the need for greater support within the industry.

The night closed with a mix of celebration and reflection. While the achievements of the winners were honored, the overarching message of the ceremony was clear—film remains one of the most powerful tools for storytelling, advocacy, and change. Whether through documentaries that expose harsh realities, narratives that give voice to the marginalized, or historical dramas that remind audiences of the past, cinema continues to be a force that shapes culture and conversation.

Animated and Visual Achievements

The 97th Academy Awards were a celebration of cinematic artistry, with the spotlight shining on films that pushed the boundaries of storytelling through animation and visual effects. This year's winners exemplified how technology, creativity, and innovation continue to transform the film industry, offering audiences breathtaking worlds, compelling characters, and unforgettable cinematic experiences.

Two films stood out in these categories—Flow, which won Best Animated Feature, and Dune: Part Two, which took home the Oscar for Best Visual Effects. Both films demonstrated how animation and cutting-edge visual effects have become essential tools for filmmakers, elevating narratives in ways previously thought impossible.

OSCARS 2025 HIGHLIGHTS

The Oscar for Best Animated Feature went to Flow, a Latvian fantasy adventure that mesmerized audiences with its unique storytelling and stunning visuals. Directed by Gints Zilbalodis, this film followed a group of animals led by a cat as they navigated a post-apocalyptic landscape devastated by a massive flood.

Unlike traditional animated films that rely on extensive dialogue and character-driven narratives, Flow took a different approach. The film used minimal dialogue, instead relying on striking visuals, atmospheric sound design, and expressive animation to convey emotion and drive the story forward. This technique immersed audiences in the world of Flow, allowing them to experience the journey through the perspective of its animal protagonists.

Visually, the film stood out for its use of soft, painterly textures and dynamic movement. The animation style blended hand-drawn elements with digital techniques, creating a dreamlike quality that set it apart from mainstream animated productions. Each frame was meticulously crafted to evoke emotion, from the serene beauty of calm waters to the chaotic intensity of storm-ravaged landscapes.

The film's director, Gints Zilbalodis, along with producers Matiss Kaza, Ron Dyens, and Gregory Zalcman, accepted the award with gratitude, emphasizing the importance of independent animation in bringing fresh and daring ideas to the screen. Their win marked a major achievement for Latvian cinema, proving that animated films from smaller studios could stand alongside big-budget productions from Hollywood giants.

Beyond its artistic achievements, Flow also carried a profound environmental message. The film's depiction of a world reshaped by rising waters served as a metaphor for climate change, subtly reminding audiences of the fragility of nature and the consequences of human impact on the planet.

Flow's victory highlighted a growing trend in the animation industry—one that embraces artistic risk-taking and storytelling innovation. In recent years, audiences have shown an increasing appetite for animated films that challenge conventional formulas, proving that animation is not limited to children's entertainment.

This year's nominees reflected this shift, with films like Wallace & Gromit: Vengeance Most Fowl, The Wild Robot, Inside Out 2, and Memoir of a Snail each offering unique takes on the medium. While mainstream studios like Pixar and DreamWorks continue to dominate the industry, independent animated films are gaining recognition for their originality, visual experimentation, and emotional depth.

The inclusion of Wallace & Gromit as a nominee was a nod to the enduring appeal of stop-motion animation, a craft that requires immense patience and precision. Meanwhile, The Wild Robot, based on the bestselling novel, combined traditional animation with cutting-edge CGI to bring its futuristic world to life. These films, along with Flow, demonstrated how animation continues to evolve, embracing both new technologies and traditional artistic techniques.

While Flow dominated the animated category, the Oscar for Best Visual Effects went to Dune: Part Two, a film that redefined the possibilities of digital effects and practical filmmaking. Directed by Denis Villeneuve, the sequel to Dune expanded upon the breathtaking world introduced in the first installment, delivering an immersive experience that captivated audiences worldwide.

The film's visual effects, overseen by the team at DNEG, were nothing short of groundbreaking. The VFX supervisors, Stephen James and Rhys Salcombe, alongside Production VFX Supervisor Paul Lambert and Special Effects Supervisor Gerd Nefzer, crafted a visually stunning world that seamlessly blended digital artistry with real-world environments. Their work on the film earned DNEG its eighth Academy Award for Visual Effects, cementing its reputation as one of the industry's leading VFX studios.

One of the most remarkable aspects of Dune: Part Two was its commitment to balancing practical effects with CGI. Rather than relying solely on computer-generated imagery, the filmmakers used large-scale physical sets, miniatures, and practical explosions to enhance realism. This approach allowed the visual effects to feel grounded, avoiding the artificial sheen that often plagues heavily CGI-reliant films.

The sandworms, one of the most iconic elements of the Dune universe, were brought to life with meticulous attention to detail. Combining practical models with advanced digital rendering, the creatures moved with a sense of weight and realism that made their on-screen presence all the more terrifying. Every grain of sand kicked up by their colossal bodies was carefully simulated, creating an awe-inspiring spectacle that immersed audiences in the harsh desert world of Arrakis.

The film's use of lighting and shadow also played a crucial role in enhancing its visual impact. Cinematographer Greig Fraser, who previously worked on Dune: Part One, employed innovative techniques to create a sense of scale and depth, making the vast desert landscapes feel both beautiful and unforgiving. Whether capturing the blinding glare of the sun or the eerie glow of Arrakis' nighttime battles, the film's visual language reinforced the epic nature of the story.

The success of Dune: Part Two underscored the importance of visual effects in modern filmmaking. As audiences become more sophisticated and demand increasingly immersive experiences, filmmakers must constantly push the boundaries of what is possible on screen.

In recent years, advancements in AI-driven animation, real-time rendering, and virtual production techniques have revolutionized the industry. Films like Avatar: The Way of Water and The Mandalorian have demonstrated the potential of virtual production stages, where LED walls replace traditional green screens, allowing actors to interact with digital environments in real-time. This technology not only enhances performances but also streamlines the filmmaking process, reducing the need for extensive post-production work.

However, despite these advancements, Dune: Part Two proved that practical effects still have a crucial role to play. By blending old-school filmmaking techniques with modern VFX, the film achieved a level of authenticity that resonated with both critics and audiences. This hybrid approach is likely to influence future blockbusters, encouraging directors to find a balance between physical and digital effects.

The triumphs of Flow and Dune: Part Two at the Oscars represented more than just technical achievements—they reflected a broader shift in the film industry toward embracing artistic diversity and innovation.

For Flow, the win signified a major milestone for independent animation, proving that smaller studios could compete with industry giants on the world stage. It also reinforced the idea that animated films could tackle complex themes and artistic storytelling without conforming to mainstream expectations.

Meanwhile, Dune: Part Two's victory in the visual effects category highlighted the growing demand for films that prioritize authenticity and craftsmanship. Rather than relying solely on CGI spectacle, audiences are showing an appreciation for films that integrate practical filmmaking techniques with digital artistry.

Best Dressed Celebrities at the Event

Once the Oscars ceremony concluded, the celebrations continued at various exclusive Vanity Fair after-parties across Hollywood. These events provided celebrities with the perfect opportunity to showcase a different side of their style—one that was often bolder, riskier, and more fashion-forward than their red-carpet looks. This year's after-parties were a dazzling display of haute couture, vintage masterpieces, and cutting-edge fashion.

One of the biggest trends of the evening was the resurgence of vintage couture. More and more celebrities are turning to archival designs, proving that fashion is cyclical and that timeless pieces never lose their charm.

Kendall Jenner embraced this trend in a Mugler archive dress, crafted from a unique rubber lace that hugged her figure perfectly. Margot Robbie, who spent much of the year promoting Barbie in pink ensembles, made a dramatic switch by donning a gold Mugler corset from the Spring/Summer 1996 collection. This bold and structured piece instantly became one of the night's standout looks.

Kaia Gerber also went vintage, stepping out in a cream-colored Valentino gown, exuding effortless grace. Meanwhile, Mikey Madison took inspiration from the golden age of Hollywood in a recreation of Dior's "Salzburg" Fall/Winter 1956-1957 Haute Couture gown, proving that some styles remain iconic through the decades.

The sheer dress trend dominated the evening, with multiple stars embracing see-through fabrics and intricate detailing. Zoë Kravitz made a bold statement in a long-sleeve black Saint Laurent gown with illusion netting, strategically designed to create a dramatic yet elegant effect. Olivia Wilde followed suit, opting for an almost entirely sheer gown, layered over matching undergarments to maintain a delicate balance between edgy and sophisticated.

Another trend that turned heads was metallic fabrics and sequins, adding a futuristic edge to the night's fashion. Selena Gomez radiated confidence in a black strapless, liquid-sequin Armani Privé gown, a dress that seemed to shimmer with every movement. Jennifer Lopez, never one to shy away from glamour, embodied pure opulence in a gold Tom Ford gown, reminiscent of an Oscar statuette itself.

Custom-designed gowns remain a favorite among Hollywood's elite, with many stars opting for one-of-a-kind creations tailored to perfection. Mary J. Blige stunned in a custom Gaurav Gupta gown, featuring dramatic sculptural elements that added an air of royalty to her look. Sydney Sweeney, embracing her love for vintage-inspired fashion, turned heads in a blush chainmail gown by Miu Miu, complete with a daring keyhole neckline.

Meanwhile, Demi Moore opted for a custom Gucci gown, emphasizing sleek lines and a modern silhouette. Cynthia Erivo, known for her fearless fashion choices, dazzled in a

Vivienne Westwood Couture corseted dress, blending historical craftsmanship with contemporary elegance.

While some stars embraced bold colors and embellishments, others relied on timeless black and white ensembles to make a statement. Kim Kardashian made an impact in a minimalist white Balenciaga gown, featuring an exaggerated skirt that added drama without excess detail. Lindsay Lohan, embracing Old Hollywood vibes, chose a white custom Balenciaga column gown, pairing it with a striking emerald necklace for a regal touch.

On the darker side of the spectrum, Christina Ricci exuded gothic elegance in a sheer black dress with plunging embellishments, while Gabrielle Union made a sophisticated entrance in a black Carolina Herrera gown with 3D gold detailing, pairing it with Tiffany & Co. jewels for extra sparkle.

While women's gowns often steal the show, the men at this year's after-parties proved that menswear is far from boring. Timothée Chalamet, known for his daring style, swapped his Oscars yellow tuxedo for a sleek Tom Ford suit, accessorized with Cartier jewelry. Drew Starkey and Joe Locke also impressed in tailored Saint Laurent ensembles, embracing sharp silhouettes and refined elegance.

Matt Bomer, never one to disappoint on the fashion front, stood out in a three-piece tuxedo paired with a patterned scarf, adding an extra touch of personality. Meanwhile, Jeff Bezos and Dwyane Wade embraced classic black-tie looks, proving that a well-fitted tuxedo will always remain a staple of Hollywood's biggest nights.

Couples brought their A-game to the after-party scene, coordinating looks that complemented each other perfectly. Katy Perry and Orlando Bloom embraced a romantic aesthetic, with Perry dazzling in a strapless Miss Sohee gown while Bloom opted for a classic black tuxedo. Gabrielle Union and Dwyane Wade took a similar approach, appearing in matching black ensembles, with Union's strapless Carolina Herrera gown accented by intricate gold embellishments.

New couple Timothée Chalamet and Kylie Jenner attended separately but were both fashion highlights of the evening. Chalamet's sleek suit exuded effortless cool, while Jenner stunned in a low-cut lace bustier gown by Ashi Studio, adding a touch of dark romance to the event.

The 2025 Oscars after-parties proved once again that Hollywood's fashion elite know how to make a statement. Whether embracing vintage treasures, custom couture, or sheer and metallic trends, the stars delivered a night of unforgettable looks. Some opted for classic elegance, while others pushed the boundaries of fashion, ensuring that this year's post-Oscars celebrations would be remembered as one of the most stylish in history.

Unexpected Wins and Snubs

The 97th Academy Awards were filled with surprises, shocking wins, and unexpected losses. While some of the night's biggest winners were widely predicted, others left audiences and industry experts stunned. Films that were expected to dominate certain categories walked away nearly empty-handed, while underdogs took home some of the most prestigious awards.

From A Complete Unknown going home without a single win to Flow unexpectedly taking Best Animated Feature, this year's Oscars proved that nothing is certain in Hollywood. Let's take a closer look at the unexpected wins and the most talked-about snubs of the night.

One of the biggest surprises of the evening was A Complete Unknown, the Bob Dylan biopic starring Timothée Chalamet, walking away with nothing. The film was nominated in eight categories, including Best Actor,

Best Adapted Screenplay, and Best Cinematography, yet failed to secure a single win.

Chalamet, who was considered a strong contender for Best Actor, lost to Adrien Brody for The Brutalist. This marked the second time in recent years that a biopic about a legendary musician failed to win any awards, following Elvis's similar fate two years ago. Despite high expectations, A Complete Unknown was completely shut out, proving that even the most celebrated films can falter when it comes to Oscar night.

Going into the ceremony with 13 nominations, Emilia Pérez was expected to be one of the biggest winners of the night. However, the Netflix crime musical managed to take home only two awards—Best Supporting Actress for Zoe Saldaña and Best Original Song for "El Mal." This made it the most nominated film in Oscar history to win so few awards, breaking the previous record held by The Curious Case of Benjamin Button, which won three of its 13 nominations in 2009.

Many believed that Emilia Pérez would take home the Oscar for Best International Feature, but that award went to I'm Still Here. The film's loss in this category was particularly surprising, as it had been heavily favored to win.

One of the most talked-about moments of the night was the Best Actress category. Demi Moore, who had been sweeping awards season for her role in The Substance, was widely expected to win her first Oscar. However, in a shocking upset, Mikey Madison took home the award for her performance in Anora.

Moore had won the Golden Globe, Critics Choice Award, and SAG Award leading up to the Oscars, making her the frontrunner. But Anora had been gaining momentum, and Madison's win marked a significant moment for the film, which went on to win five awards, including Best Picture.

While Madison's performance was widely praised, Moore's loss was unexpected, especially given her long career and critical acclaim for The Substance. Some saw it as another example of the Academy's reluctance to fully embrace the horror genre, as the film was primarily recognized for its makeup and hairstyling rather than its performances.

Legendary songwriter Diane Warren extended her Oscar losing streak, bringing her total to 16 nominations without a win. Her song "The Journey" from The Six Triple Eight lost to Emilia Pérez's "El Mal."

Despite receiving an honorary Academy Award in 2023 for her contributions to music, Warren has yet to win a competitive Oscar. She now shares the record for the most nominations without a win with sound mixing specialist Greg P. Russell.

A surprising snub came in the form of Nosferatu, which had received strong critical acclaim and multiple nominations. The gothic horror film, which had impressed with its production design and cinematography, failed to win any awards. Given the Academy's history of overlooking horror films, this outcome was disappointing but not entirely unexpected.

One of the biggest upsets of the night came in the Best Animated Feature category, where Flow defeated heavyweights like Inside Out 2 and The Wild Robot. Many had predicted that The Wild Robot, which had been critically acclaimed and had performed well throughout awards season, would take the Oscar. However, Flow's stunning visuals and unique storytelling secured it the win, making it the first Latvian film to win in this category.

This marked a major milestone for independent animation, proving that smaller studios could compete with Hollywood giants like Disney and Pixar.

Sean Baker made history by tying Walt Disney's 1954 record for most Oscars won in a single night. Baker had been expected to take home three Oscars for Anora—Best Picture, Best Director, and Best Original Screenplay. However, when he also won Best Film Editing, he matched Disney's long-standing record.

OSCARS 2025 HIGHLIGHTS

This achievement cemented Anora's status as the night's biggest winner, as the film took home five Oscars in total.

Another major surprise came when I'm Still Here won Best International Feature over Emilia Pérez. Many had assumed that Emilia Pérez would take the award, given its strong presence in other categories. However, I'm Still Here, a Brazilian drama about a woman seeking justice for her husband's disappearance during the country's dictatorship, managed to pull off the upset.

The film had received critical acclaim but had not been expected to beat Emilia Pérez, making its win one of the most unexpected moments of the night.

While Dune: Part Two winning Best Visual Effects was not entirely unexpected, it was a surprise that it beat Wicked, which had been considered a strong contender in multiple technical categories.

The Academy has a history of using the visual effects category to recognize large-scale blockbusters that don't necessarily fit into the Best Picture race, and Dune: Part Two fit that pattern perfectly. The film's seamless integration of CGI and practical effects made it a deserving winner, but Wicked's loss in this category was surprising given its elaborate production design.

Perhaps the most politically charged moment of the night came when No Other Land won Best Documentary Feature. The film, which documents the destruction of Palestinian villages in the occupied West Bank, had faced difficulties securing distribution in the United States.

During their acceptance speech, the filmmakers made a powerful statement about the ongoing human rights crisis in the region, calling for international action. The win was significant not just for its content but for the fact that it came despite a lack of major studio backing.

The Oscars and the Future of Cinema

The 97th Academy Awards showcased more than just the best films of the year; it reflected the ongoing transformation of the film industry and offered a glimpse into the future of cinema. The Oscars have always been a measure of where Hollywood stands, highlighting trends, recognizing new talent, and setting the stage for what audiences can expect in the years ahead. With independent films gaining momentum, streaming platforms challenging traditional distribution models, and discussions about diversity and inclusion shaping industry decisions, this year's ceremony marked a turning point.

One of the biggest takeaways from the 2025 Oscars was the triumph of independent filmmaking. Anora, directed by Sean Baker, won Best Picture, Best Director, and two other major awards, proving that small-budget films with strong storytelling can stand toe-to-toe with blockbuster productions. Baker's win reaffirmed that audiences are craving fresh, authentic narratives that don't rely on high production costs or extensive special effects. His speech, where he emphasized the importance of keeping cinema alive in theaters, resonated with many who worry about the decline of traditional movie-going.

The rise of independent films at the Oscars is a reflection of a larger shift in the industry. In recent years, audiences have grown tired of franchise-heavy lineups dominated by sequels, prequels, and superhero films. While big-budget productions still have a place in Hollywood, the success of Anora and other indie films shows that there is room for original stories that take risks. Streaming platforms have also contributed to this shift, making it easier for smaller films to reach global audiences. However, the debate over whether streaming is helping or hurting cinema continues to be a major discussion in Hollywood.

The future of cinema will likely be shaped by the balance between theatrical releases and streaming platforms. While some argue that streaming services have made films more accessible, others believe they are eroding the theatrical experience. Studios are now experimenting with hybrid release models, where films have a limited theatrical run before being made available online. This year's Oscars reflected this changing landscape, with nominees coming from both traditional studios and streaming platforms. The question now is whether theaters can remain a dominant force in an era where convenience often outweighs the desire for a communal movie-watching experience.

Another key theme at this year's ceremony was the continued push for diversity and representation. The Academy has faced criticism in the past for its lack of inclusivity, but recent years have seen a more conscious effort to recognize talent from different backgrounds. The 97th Academy Awards featured a historically diverse group of nominees, including first-time directors, international filmmakers, and actors from underrepresented communities. This progress is promising, but the industry still has a long way to go in ensuring that all voices are heard.

OSCARS 2025 HIGHLIGHTS

The future of cinema depends on expanding the range of stories being told. Audiences today are more aware than ever of the need for authentic representation, and they are pushing for films that reflect different cultures, perspectives, and experiences. The success of films like Emilia Pérez, which received multiple nominations, proves that international cinema is becoming more integrated into mainstream Hollywood. Moving forward, the Oscars will likely continue to highlight films from diverse voices, further breaking down the barriers that have historically limited the industry.

Technology is also playing a major role in shaping the future of filmmaking. Advancements in visual effects, virtual production, and artificial intelligence are changing how movies are made. While some fear that AI-generated content could threaten creativity, many filmmakers are finding ways to use technology to enhance storytelling rather than replace it. The Oscars have always celebrated technical achievements, and future ceremonies may recognize innovations that redefine how films are produced.

At the same time, there is growing concern about maintaining the artistic integrity of cinema in an industry that is becoming increasingly data-driven. Studios now rely heavily on algorithms and audience metrics to determine which films get made, which can sometimes stifle creativity. The challenge for the next generation of filmmakers will be finding a balance between artistic vision and commercial viability. The Oscars will continue to be a space where artistic risks are rewarded, but the industry must ensure that original voices are not lost in the pursuit of market trends.

The role of film festivals and awards shows in shaping the future of cinema remains crucial. Events like Cannes, Sundance, and the Toronto International Film Festival continue to be launching pads for groundbreaking films, often influencing which movies gain traction during awards season. The Oscars, despite occasional criticisms, still hold significant cultural weight, and their recognition can propel a film or a filmmaker to greater success. The challenge moving forward will be ensuring that the awards remain relevant and continue to evolve with the changing industry.

Conclusion

The 97th Academy Awards highlighted a turning point for the film industry, showcasing the power of independent cinema, the evolving role of streaming platforms, and the ongoing push for diversity in storytelling. Sean Baker's triumph with Anora reinforced that bold, character-driven narratives can stand alongside major studio productions, proving that audiences still value originality and authenticity.

As the industry moves forward, the balance between theatrical releases and digital platforms will continue to shape how films reach audiences. The push for greater representation will drive more inclusive storytelling, ensuring that voices from different backgrounds receive the recognition they deserve. Advancements in technology will present new opportunities and challenges, but the heart of filmmaking—compelling stories and visionary directors—will always remain at the core of cinema's future.

The Oscars remain a symbol of excellence, setting the standard for what is celebrated in Hollywood. If this year's ceremony is any indication, the future of cinema is one where creativity thrives, where new voices are embraced, and where the magic of storytelling continues to captivate audiences worldwide.

Printed in Dunstable, United Kingdom

67613696R00060